THE
Picnic
BOOK

STYLISH AND SIMPLE RECIPES
FOR OUTDOOR ENTERTAINING

CHRISTINE FRANCE

HERMES
HOUSE

This Paperback edition published by Hermes House
an imprint of
Anness Publishing Limited
Hermes House
88-89 Blackfriars Road
London SE1 8HA

A CIP catalogue record for this book is available from the British Library

ISBN 1 84038 721 1

Publisher: Joanna Lorenz
Editor: Sarah Ainley
Copy Editor: Beverley Jollands
Designer: Nigel Partridge
Illustrations: Madeleine David and Lucinda Ganderton
Photographers: Karl Adamson, Steve Baxter, John Freeman, Michelle Garrett,
Amanda Heywood, Patrick McLeavey, Debbie Patterson and Juliet Piddington
Recipes: Carla Capalbo, Jacqueline Clark, Carole Clements, Tessa Evelegh,
Joanna Farrow, Silvana Franco, Soheila Kimberley, Katherine Richmond and
Elizabeth Wolf-Cohen

For all recipes, quantities are given in both metric and imperial measures,
and, where appropriate, measures are also given in standard cups and spoons.
Follow one set, but not a mixture, because they are not interchangeable.

Printed and bound in Singapore

© Anness Publishing Limited 1998
Updated © 2000
1 3 5 7 9 10 8 6 4 2

THE
₽ICNIC
BOOK

CONTENTS

. . .

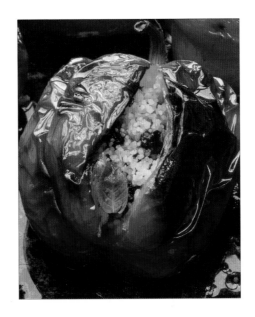

INTRODUCTION

—✦—

Everything tastes better outdoors, and picnics – whether in

the garden, at the seaside or in a grassy meadow – are a great pleasure

both to organize and to take part in, as long as the weather is kind.

If you have a portable barbecue you can take it along with you and

make the food twice as exciting, but take care that you light it in

a safe place and clear up carefully afterwards. Food for barbecuing

can be transported in its marinade, all ready to be popped on the grill.

Kitchenware companies have responded quickly to the popularity

of picnics, and there is now a vast range of equipment available to

the dedicated picnicker. There are suitable containers for every type

and shape of food, some with separate compartments for sauces

and dressings, and chiller boxes to carry them in. Bear in mind that

while better insulated containers have improved food safety, there's

no room for complacency: there's little point in keeping food chilled if

you later leave it standing in the sunshine for several hours. Pack

any uneaten food away quickly: you can always get it out again.

The final section of the book offers inspirations for special summer

meals, barbecues and garden parties at home, including some original

and delicious ideas for party drinks.

STARTERS AND SNACKS

POTATO SKINS WITH CAJUN DIP

As an alternative to deep frying, grilling potato skins crisps them up in no time. This spicy dip makes the perfect partner.

INGREDIENTS

4 large baking potatoes
olive oil for brushing
250ml/8fl oz/1 cup natural yogurt
2 garlic cloves, crushed
10ml/2 tsp tomato paste
5ml/1 tsp green chilli paste or
1 small green chilli, chopped
2.5ml/½ tsp celery salt
salt and freshly ground black
pepper

SERVES 4

1 Bake or microwave the potatoes until tender. Cut them in half and scoop out the flesh, leaving a thin layer of potato on the skins. The scooped out potato can be reserved in the fridge or freezer for another meal.

2 Cut each potato shell in half again and lightly brush the skins with olive oil. Cook under a medium-hot grill for 4–5 minutes, or until crisp.

3 Mix together the remaining ingredients in a bowl to make the dip. Serve the potato skins with the Cajun dip on the side.

Cook's Tip
If you don't have any chilli paste or fresh chillies, add one or two drops of hot pepper sauce to the dip instead.

VEGETABLES WITH TAPENADE AND HERB AIOLI

A beautiful platter of summer vegetables served with one or two interesting sauces makes a really appetizing and informal starter, which is perfect for picnics as it can all be prepared in advance.

INGREDIENTS

2 red peppers, cut into wide strips
30ml/2 tbsp olive oil
225g/8oz new potatoes
115g/4oz green beans
225g/8oz baby carrots
225g/8oz young asparagus
12 quails' eggs
fresh herbs, to garnish
coarse salt, for sprinkling

FOR THE TAPENADE
175g/6oz/1½ cups stoned black olives
50g/2oz can anchovy fillets, drained
30ml/2 tbsp capers
120ml/4fl oz/½ cup olive oil
finely grated rind of 1 lemon
15ml/1 tbsp brandy (optional)
freshly ground black pepper

FOR THE HERB AIOLI
5 garlic cloves, crushed
2 egg yolks
5ml/1 tsp Dijon mustard
10ml/2 tsp white wine vinegar
250ml/8fl oz/1 cup light olive oil
45ml/3 tbsp chopped mixed fresh herbs, such as chervil, parsley and tarragon
30ml/2 tbsp chopped watercress
salt and freshly ground black pepper

SERVES 6

1 To make the tapenade, finely chop the olives, anchovies and capers and beat together with the oil, lemon rind and brandy, if using. (Alternatively, lightly process the ingredients in a blender or food processor.)

2 Season with pepper and blend in a little more oil if the mixture seems very dry. Transfer to a serving dish.

3 To make the aïoli, beat together the garlic, egg yolks, mustard and vinegar. Gradually blend in the olive oil, a drop at a time, whisking well until thick and smooth.

4 Stir in the mixed herbs and watercress. Season with salt and pepper to taste, adding a little more vinegar if necessary. Cover with clear film and chill until ready to serve.

Cook's Tip
Any leftover tapenade is delicious tossed with pasta or spread on to warm toast. If you are making this dish as part of a picnic, allow the vegetables to cool before packing in an airtight container. Pack the quails' eggs in their original box.

5 Brush the peppers with oil and grill on a hot barbecue or under a hot grill until just beginning to char.

6 Cook the potatoes in a large pan of boiling, salted water until tender. Add the beans and carrots and blanch for 1 minute. Add the asparagus and cook for a further 30 seconds. Drain the vegetables. Cook the quails' eggs in boiling water for 2 minutes.

7 Arrange all the vegetables, eggs and sauces on a serving platter. Garnish with fresh herbs and serve with coarse salt, for sprinkling.

CRUDITES

° ° °

Serve a colourful selection of raw vegetables as a refreshing starter for outdoor meals.

RAW VEGETABLE PLATTER

INGREDIENTS

2 red or yellow peppers, sliced
lengthways
225g/8oz fresh baby corn,
blanched
1 chicory head (red or white),
trimmed and leaves separated
175–225g/6–8oz thin asparagus,
trimmed and blanched
small bunch radishes, trimmed
175g/6oz cherry tomatoes
12 quail's eggs, boiled for
3 minutes, drained, refreshed and
peeled
aïoli or tapenade,
for dipping

SERVES 6–8

Arrange a selection of prepared
vegetables, chosen from the list above,
on a serving plate with your chosen
dip. Keep covered until ready to serve.

TOMATO AND CUCUMBER SALAD

INGREDIENTS

1 medium cucumber, peeled and
thinly sliced
30ml/2 tbsp white wine vinegar
90ml/3fl oz/$^1/_3$ cup crème fraîche or
soured cream
30ml/2 tbsp chopped fresh mint
4 or 5 ripe tomatoes, sliced
salt and freshly ground black
pepper

SERVES 4–6

Place the cucumber in a bowl, sprinkle
with a little salt and 15ml/1 tbsp of the
vinegar and toss with 5 or 6 ice cubes.
Chill for 1 hour, then rinse, drain and
pat dry. Return to the bowl to stir in
the cream, pepper and mint, then pack
in a box. At the picnic site, arrange
the tomato slices on a plate, sprinkle
with the remaining vinegar and spoon
the cucumber slices into the centre.

Cook's Tip
Any leftover vegetables can
be used in soups or stir-fries,
even if they have already
been dressed.

CARROT AND ORANGE SALAD

INGREDIENTS

1 garlic clove, crushed
grated rind and juice of 1 unwaxed
orange
30–45ml/2–3 tbsp groundnut oil
450g/1lb carrots, cut into very fine
julienne strips
30–45ml/2–3 tbsp chopped fresh
parsley
salt and freshly ground black
pepper

SERVES 4–6

Rub around a bowl with the garlic
clove, leaving the clove in the bowl.
Add the orange rind and juice, and
season with salt and freshly ground
pepper. Whisk in the groundnut oil
until blended, then remove the garlic
clove. Add the carrots and half of the
fresh parsley and toss to mix. Pack the
salad in a box, garnished with parsley.

AIOLI

Put 4 peeled garlic cloves (more or less can be added, to taste) in a bowl with a pinch of salt, and crush with the back of a spoon. Add 2 egg yolks and beat for 30 seconds with an electric mixer until creamy. Beat in 250ml/8fl oz/ 1 cup extra virgin olive oil, drop by drop. As the mixture thickens, the oil can be added in a thin stream. Thin the sauce with lemon juice, if necessary, and season. Chill for up to 2 days. Pack in a screw-topped jar to transport to the picnic and stir before serving.

TAPENADE

Put 200g/7oz stoned black olives, 6 anchovy fillets, 30ml/2 tbsp capers, rinsed, 1 or 2 garlic cloves, 5ml/1 tsp fresh thyme, 15ml/1 tbsp Dijon mustard, the juice of half a lemon, freshly ground black pepper and, if you like, 15ml/1 tbsp brandy in a food processor and process for about 15–30 seconds until smooth, scraping down the sides of the bowl. With the machine running, pour in 60–90ml/4–6 tbsp extra virgin olive oil to make a smooth paste. Store in an airtight container.

FROM TOP LEFT: raw vegetable platter with aïoli, carrot and orange salad, tomato and cucumber salad.

HERB-STUFFED MINI VEGETABLES

These little hors d'oeuvres are ideal for picnics: prepare them in advance, wrap them individually in baking foil and pack them tightly in a box to transport to the picnic site.

INGREDIENTS

30 mini vegetables: courgettes, patty pan squashes and large button mushrooms
30ml/2 tbsp olive oil
fresh basil or parsley, to garnish

FOR THE STUFFING
30ml/2 tbsp olive oil
1 onion, finely chopped
1 garlic clove, finely chopped
115g/4oz button mushrooms, finely chopped
1 courgette, finely chopped
1 red pepper, finely chopped
65g/2½ oz/⅓ cup orzo pasta or long grain rice
90ml/6 tbsp/⅓ cup passata
2.5ml/½ tsp dried thyme
120ml/4fl oz/½ cup chicken stock
5–10ml/1–2 tsp chopped fresh basil or parsley
50g/2oz mozzarella or fontina cheese, coarsely grated
salt and freshly ground black pepper

MAKES 30

2 Stir in the pasta or rice, the passata, thyme and stock and bring to the boil, stirring. Reduce the heat and simmer for 10–12 minutes until reduced and thickened. Remove from the heat and cool slightly. Stir in the basil or parsley and the cheese.

3 Drop the courgettes and squashes into boiling water and cook for 3 minutes. Drain and refresh under cold running water. Trim the bottoms so they are flat, trim a small slice off the tops and scoop out the centres with a spoon or melon baller. Remove the stems from the mushrooms. Brush all the vegetables with olive oil.

4 Using a teaspoon, fill the vegetables with the stuffing and arrange on a rack. Grill for 10–15 minutes until the filling is hot and bubbling. Garnish with the fresh basil or parsley. The vegetables can be served either warm or cold.

1 For the stuffing, heat the oil over a medium heat in a pan. Add the onion and cook for 2 minutes until tender. Stir in the garlic, mushrooms, courgette and red pepper. Season and cook for 2 minutes until the vegetables soften.

SPICY CHICKEN WINGS

These deliciously sticky bites will appeal to adults and children alike, although younger eaters might prefer a little less chilli.

INGREDIENTS

8 plump chicken wings
2 large garlic cloves, cut into slivers
15ml/1 tbsp olive oil
15ml/1 tbsp paprika
5ml/1 tsp chilli powder
5ml/1 tsp dried oregano
salt and freshly ground black pepper
lime wedges, to serve

SERVES 4

1 Using a small sharp kitchen knife, make one or two cuts in the skin of each chicken wing and slide a sliver of garlic under the skin. Brush the wings generously with the olive oil.

2 In a large bowl, stir together the paprika, chilli powder and oregano and season with plenty of salt and pepper. Add the chicken wings and toss together until very lightly coated in the mixture.

3 Cook the chicken wings on a medium grill for 15 minutes until they are cooked through, with a blackened, crispy skin. Pack in a box, with fresh lime wedges to squeeze over before serving.

STUFFED KIBBEH

Kibbeh is a tasty Middle Eastern speciality of minced lamb and bulgar wheat, which can be shaped into patties and deep fried.

INGREDIENTS

450g/1lb lean lamb
45ml/3 tbsp olive oil
avocado slices and fresh coriander
sprigs, to serve

FOR THE KIBBEH
225g/8oz/1⅓ cups bulgur wheat
1 red chilli, seeded and roughly
chopped
1 onion, roughly chopped
salt and freshly ground black
pepper

FOR THE STUFFING
1 onion, finely chopped
50g/2oz/⅔ cup pine nuts
30ml/2 tbsp olive oil
7.5ml/1½ tsp ground allspice
60ml/4 tbsp chopped fresh
coriander

SERVES 4–6

1 Roughly cut the lamb into chunks, using a heavy kitchen knife. Process the chunks in a blender or food processor until finely minced. Divide the minced meat into two equal portions and set aside until needed.

2 To make the kibbeh, soak the bulgur wheat for 15 minutes in cold water. Drain well, then process in the blender or food processor with the chopped chilli and onion, half the meat and plenty of salt and pepper.

3 To make the stuffing, fry the onion and pine nuts in the olive oil for 5 minutes. Add the allspice and remaining minced meat and fry gently, breaking up the meat with a wooden spoon, until browned. Stir in the coriander and a little seasoning.

4 Turn the kibbeh mixture out on to a clean work surface and use your hands to shape the mixture into a cake. Divide the cake into 12 wedges.

5 Flatten one wedge in the palm of your hand and spoon a little stuffing into the centre. Bring the edges of the kibbeh over the stuffing to enclose it. Make into a firm egg-shaped mould between the palms of your hands, ensuring that the filling is completely encased. Repeat with the other kibbeh.

6 To fry the kibbeh, heat oil to a depth of 5cm/2in in a large saucepan until a few kibbeh crumbs sizzle on the surface. Lower half the kibbeh into the oil and fry for about 5 minutes until golden. Drain on kitchen paper and keep hot while frying the remainder. Allow the kibbeh to cool before packing in a tin to transport to the picnic site. Serve with avocado slices and fresh coriander sprigs.

FALAFEL

° ° °

These North African fritters are traditionally made using dried broad beans, but chick-peas are more easily available. Serve in pitta bread, with salad and garlicky yogurt.

INGREDIENTS

150g/5oz/³⁄4 cup dried chick-peas
1 large onion, roughly chopped
2 garlic cloves, roughly chopped
60ml/4 tbsp roughly chopped fresh
parsley
5ml/1 tsp cumin seeds, crushed
5ml/1 tsp coriander seeds, crushed
2.5ml/¹⁄2 tsp baking powder
salt and freshly ground black
pepper
oil for deep frying

SERVES 4

1 Put the chick-peas in a large bowl and cover with plenty of cold water. Leave to soak overnight.

2 Drain the chick-peas and cover with fresh water in a saucepan. Bring to the boil and boil rapidly for 10 minutes. Reduce the heat and simmer for about 1 hour, or until soft. Drain.

3 Place in a food processor with the onion, garlic, parsley, cumin, coriander and baking powder. Season to taste. Process to form a firm paste.

4 Shape the mixture into walnut-size balls, using your hands, and flatten them slightly. In a deep pan, heat 5cm/2in oil until a little of the mixture sizzles on the surface. Fry the falafel in batches until golden. Drain on kitchen paper before packing.

Cook's Tip
Although they can be fried in advance, falafel are at their best served warm. Wrap them in foil or pack them in an insulated container to take them on picnics.

HUMMUS BI TAHINA

Blending chick-peas with garlic, lemon and oil makes a deliciously creamy purée to serve as a dip with crudités or pitta bread.

INGREDIENTS

150g/5oz/³/4 cup dried chick-peas
juice of 2 lemons
2 garlic cloves, sliced
30ml/2 tbsp olive oil, plus extra to serve
150ml/¹/4 pint/²/3 cup tahini paste
salt and freshly ground black pepper
cayenne pepper, to serve
flat leaf parsley, to garnish

SERVES 4–6

1 Put the chick-peas in a large bowl and cover with plenty of cold water. Leave to soak overnight.

2 Drain the chick-peas and cover with fresh water in a pan. Bring to the boil and boil rapidly for 10 minutes. Reduce the heat and simmer for about 1 hour, or until soft. Drain.

3 Process the chick-peas to a purée in a food processor. Add lemon juice, garlic, olive oil and tahini and blend until creamy.

4 Season the chick-pea purée with plenty of salt and freshly ground black pepper and transfer to a serving dish. Drizzle the purée with olive oil and sprinkle lightly with cayenne pepper. Serve the dip garnished with a few flat leaf parsley sprigs.

Cook's Tip

If you do not have time to soak dried chick-peas, canned chick-peas can be used instead. Allow two 400g/14oz cans and drain them thoroughly.

QUICK SEAFOOD PIZZA

Make four mini pizzas or one large one with the same quantities of ingredients.
If you are short of time, use a pizza-base mix instead of making the dough.

INGREDIENTS

FOR THE PIZZA BASE
5ml/1 tsp easy-blend yeast
450g/1lb/4 cups strong bread flour
15ml/1tbsp sugar
5ml/1tsp sea salt
300ml/½ pint/1¼ cups
lukewarm water
30ml/2tbsp extra virgin olive oil

FOR THE FISH TOPPING
1 onion, finely chopped
800g/1¾ lb canned or fresh plum
tomatoes, chopped
salt and freshly ground black
pepper
15ml/1 tbsp chopped fresh thyme
15ml/1 tbsp olive oil
115g/4oz cherry tomatoes
12 fresh anchovy fillets, or 1 can
anchovy fillets, drained
8 fresh, peeled prawns
a few sprigs of fresh thyme,
to garnish
SERVES 4

1 Preheat the oven to 200°C/
400°F/Gas 6. Stir the easy-blend yeast
into the flour in a large mixing bowl.
Add the sugar and sea salt and blend
together well.

2 Add the water and olive oil to the
bowl, and stir to make a firm dough.

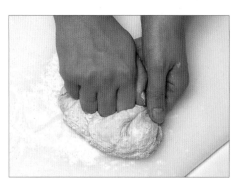

3 Knead the dough for about 10
minutes. Cover and leave in a warm
place until it has doubled in size.

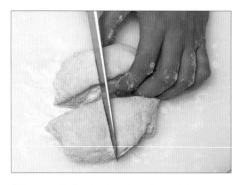

4 Knock back the dough and knead
for 5 minutes, then cut the dough into
four. Shape each of the four pieces of
dough into 13cm/5in circles.

5 Fry the onion until soft. Add the
canned tomatoes, seasoning and thyme
and simmer for 15 minutes. Brush the
pizza bases with olive oil and cook in
the preheated oven, oiled side down,
for about 6–8 minutes, until firm and
golden underneath. Oil the uncooked
side and turn the pizzas over.

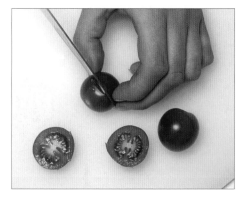

6 Cut the cherry tomatoes in half.
Assemble each of the pizzas with a
spoonful of the sauce, a couple of
anchovy fillets and prawns and the
cherry tomatoes. Return to the oven
and cook for a further 8–10 minutes
until crispy. Scatter a few fresh sprigs
of thyme on top of the pizzas. Allow
to cool before packing.

Variation
Add your favourite seafood,
such as fresh or canned mussels,
to the topping.

TANDOORI CHICKEN STICKS

These aromatic chicken pieces are traditionally baked in the special clay oven known as a tandoor. They are equally delicious served hot or cold, and make an irresistible picnic snack.

INGREDIENTS

450g/1lb boneless, skinless chicken breasts

FOR THE CORIANDER YOGURT
250ml/8fl oz/1 cup natural yogurt
30ml/2 tbsp whipping cream
1/2 cucumber, peeled, seeded and finely chopped
15–30ml/1–2 tbsp fresh chopped coriander or mint
salt and freshly ground black pepper

FOR THE MARINADE
175ml/6fl oz/3/4 cup natural yogurt
5ml/1 tsp garam masala or curry powder
1.5ml/1/4 tsp ground cumin
1.5ml/1/4 tsp ground coriander
1.5ml/1/4 tsp cayenne pepper (or to taste)
5ml/1 tsp tomato purée
1–2 garlic cloves, finely chopped
2.5cm/1in piece fresh root ginger, finely chopped
grated zest and juice of 1/2 lemon
15–30ml/1–2 tbsp fresh chopped coriander or mint

MAKES ABOUT 25

2 To prepare the marinade, place all the ingredients in a food processor and process until smooth. Pour into a shallow dish.

3 Freeze the chicken breasts for 5 minutes to firm them, then slice in half horizontally. Cut the slices into 2cm/3/4in strips and add to the marinade. Toss to coat well. Cover with clear film and chill for 6–8 hours or overnight.

4 Drain the chicken pieces and arrange on a foil-lined baking sheet, scrunching up the chicken slightly to make wavy shapes. Cook under a hot grill until brown and cooked through, turning once. Allow the chicken to cool, then thread on cocktail sticks or short skewers and pack into a box. Serve with the coriander yogurt.

1 For the coriander yogurt, combine all the ingredients in a bowl. Season, cover and chill until ready to serve.

RED ONION GALETTES

If non-vegetarians are to eat these pretty puff pastry tarts, you can scatter some chopped anchovies over them before baking to add extra piquancy.

INGREDIENTS

60–75ml/4–5 tbsp olive oil
500g/1¼ lb red onions, sliced
1 garlic clove, crushed
30ml/2 tbsp chopped fresh mixed herbs, such as thyme, parsley and basil
225g/8oz ready-made puff pastry
15ml/1 tbsp sun-dried tomato paste
freshly ground black pepper
fresh thyme sprigs, to garnish

SERVES 4

1 Heat 30ml/2 tbsp oil in a frying pan and add the onions and garlic. Cover and cook gently for 15–20 minutes, until soft. Stir in the herbs. Preheat the oven to 200°C/400°F/Gas 6.

2 Divide the pastry into four and roll out each piece to a 15cm/6in round. Flute the edges, prick all over with a fork and place on baking sheets.

3 Chill the rounds, on the baking sheets, in the fridge for 10 minutes. Mix 15ml/1 tbsp of the remaining olive oil with the sun-dried tomato paste and spread over the pastry rounds, to within about 1cm/½ in of the edge.

4 Spread the onion mixture over the pastry and season with pepper. Drizzle over a little oil, then place the baking sheets in the preheated oven for 15 minutes, until crisp. Serve garnished with thyme sprigs.

MEAT AND POULTRY DISHES

FARMHOUSE PIZZA

Pizza makes a wonderfully appetizing picnic food. Shape the dough to fit your baking sheet and allow the cooked pizza to cool completely before packing.

INGREDIENTS
90ml/6 tbsp olive oil
225g/8oz button mushrooms, sliced
300g/11oz packet pizza-base mix
300ml/¹/₂ pint/1¹/₄ cups tomato sauce
300g/11oz mozzarella cheese, thinly sliced
115g/4oz wafer-thin smoked ham slices
6 bottled artichoke hearts in oil, drained and sliced
50g/2oz can anchovy fillets, drained and halved lengthways
10 stoned black olives, halved
30ml/2 tbsp chopped fresh oregano
45ml/3 tbsp freshly grated Parmesan cheese
freshly ground black pepper

SERVES 8

1 Preheat the oven to 200°C/400°F/ Gas 6. Heat 30ml/2 tbsp oil in a pan and fry the mushrooms. Leave to cool.

2 Make up the pizza dough according to the directions on the packet. Roll it out on a floured surface to a 30 × 25cm/12 × 10in rectangle. Brush with oil and place, oiled side down, on a baking sheet in the oven. Cook for 6 minutes until firm.

3 Brush the cooked side of the dough with oil and turn over. Spread over the tomato sauce and arrange the sliced mozzarella on top. Scrunch up the smoked ham and arrange on top with the artichoke hearts, anchovies and cooked mushrooms.

4 Dot with the halved olives, then sprinkle over the fresh oregano and Parmesan. Drizzle over the remaining olive oil and season with black pepper. Return to the oven and cook for a further 8–10 minutes, or until the dough is golden brown and crisp.

NEW ORLEANS STEAK SALAD

The New Orleans "Poor Boy" started life in the Creole community, as a sandwich filled with leftover scraps. This salad, made with tender beef steak, is a variation on the sandwich.

INGREDIENTS

*4 sirloin or rump steaks,
about 175g/6oz each
1 escarole lettuce
1 bunch watercress
4 tomatoes, quartered
4 large gherkins, sliced
4 spring onions, sliced
4 canned artichoke hearts, halved
175g/6oz button mushrooms,
sliced
12 green olives
120ml/4fl oz/½ cup French dressing
salt and freshly ground black
pepper*

SERVES 4

1 Season the steaks with plenty of black pepper and cook under a hot grill for 4–6 minutes, turning once, until medium-rare. Cover and leave the steaks to cool. When cool, slice each steak diagonally.

2 Combine the salad leaves with all the ingredients except the steak. Pack the French dressing separately.

3 At the picnic site, divide the salad between 4 plates, add the dressing and arrange the steak slices over the salad.

THAI BEEF SALAD

A hearty salad of beef and crunchy vegetables, laced with a tangy chilli and lime dressing.
The meat gives a truly delicious flavour to the salad.

INGREDIENTS

2 sirloin steaks, about
225g/8oz each
1 red onion, finely sliced
1/2 cucumber, finely sliced into
matchsticks
1 stalk lemon grass, finely chopped
30ml/2 tbsp chopped spring onions
juice of 2 limes
15–30ml/1–2 tbsp Thai fish sauce
2–4 red chillies, finely sliced, to
garnish
fresh coriander, Chinese mustard
cress and mint leaves, to garnish

SERVES 4

1 Pan-fry the beef steaks until they are medium-rare. Allow the steaks to cool completely.

2 When the steaks have cooled, slice them thinly, using a heavy knife, and pack the slices into a box.

3 Add the sliced onion, cucumber matchsticks and chopped lemon grass. Add the spring onions.

4 At the picnic site, toss and season with lime juice and Thai fish sauce. Serve garnished with the chillies, coriander, mustard cress and mint.

SPICED BEEF SATAY

Tender strips of steak threaded on skewers and spiced with the characteristic flavours of Indonesia are popular with everyone.

INGREDIENTS
450g/1lb rump steak, cut in 1cm/1/2
in strips
5ml/1 tsp coriander seeds, dry fried
and ground
2.5ml/1/2 tsp cumin seeds, dry fried
and ground
5ml/1 tsp tamarind pulp
1 small onion
2 garlic cloves
15ml/1 tbsp brown sugar
15ml/1 tbsp dark soy sauce
salt

TO SERVE
cucumber chunks
lemon or lime wedges
Sambal Kecap

MAKES 18 SKEWERS

1 Mix the meat and spices in a large non-metallic bowl. Soak the tamarind pulp in 75ml/3fl oz/1/3 cup water.

2 Strain the tamarind and reserve the juice. Put the onion, garlic, tamarind juice, sugar and soy sauce in a food processor and blend well.

3 Pour the marinade over the meat and spices in the bowl and toss well together. Leave for at least 1 hour.

4 Meanwhile, soak some bamboo skewers in water to prevent them from burning while cooking. Thread 5 or 6 pieces of meat on to each skewer and sprinkle with salt. Cook under a medium-hot grill, turning the skewers frequently and basting with the marinade, until the meat is tender.

5 Serve with cucumber chunks and wedges of lemon or lime for squeezing over the meat. Sambal Kecap makes a traditional accompaniment.

SAMBAL KECAP
Mix 1 fresh red chilli,
seeded and finely chopped,
2 crushed garlic cloves and
60ml/4 tbsp dark soy sauce with
20ml/4 tsp lemon juice and
30ml/2 tbsp hot water in a bowl.
Leave to stand for 30 minutes
before packing.

STUFFED AUBERGINES WITH LAMB

∘ ∘ ∘

Minced lamb and aubergines go together beautifully. This is an attractive dish,
using different coloured peppers in the lightly spiced stuffing mixture.

INGREDIENTS

2 medium aubergines
30ml/2 tbsp vegetable oil
1 medium onion, sliced
5ml/1 tsp grated fresh root ginger
5ml/1 tsp chilli powder
1 garlic clove, crushed
1.5ml/¼ tsp turmeric
5ml/1 tsp salt
5ml/1 tsp ground coriander
1 medium tomato, chopped
350g/12oz minced lean lamb
1 medium green pepper, roughly
chopped
1 medium orange pepper, roughly
chopped
30ml/2 tbsp chopped fresh
coriander

FOR THE GARNISH
½ onion, sliced
2 cherry tomatoes, quartered
fresh coriander sprigs

SERVES 4

1 Cut the aubergines in half
lengthways with a heavy knife. Scoop
out most of the flesh and reserve it for
another dish. Brush the shells with a
little vegetable oil.

2 In a medium saucepan, heat 15ml/
1 tbsp oil and fry the sliced onion until
golden brown. Stir in the grated ginger,
chilli powder, garlic, turmeric, salt and
ground coriander. Add the chopped
tomato, lower the heat and cook for
about 5 minutes, stirring continuously.

3 Add the minced lamb to the
saucepan and continue to cook over
a medium heat for about 7–10 minutes.
Stir in the chopped fresh peppers and
the fresh coriander.

4 Spoon the lamb mixture into the
aubergine shells and brush the edges
of the shells with the remaining oil.
Cook under a medium grill for
15–20 minutes until cooked through.
Allow to cool before packing. Garnish
at the picnic site, before serving.

TURKEY ROLLS WITH GAZPACHO SAUCE

This Spanish-style recipe uses quick-cooking turkey steaks, but you could also cook veal escalopes in the same way.

INGREDIENTS

4 turkey breast steaks
15ml/1 tbsp red pesto
4 chorizo sausages
15ml/1 tbsp olive oil
salt and freshly ground black pepper

FOR THE GAZPACHO SAUCE
1 green pepper, chopped
1 red pepper, chopped
7.5cm/3in piece cucumber
1 medium tomato
1 garlic clove
45ml/3 tbsp olive oil
15ml/1 tbsp red wine vinegar

SERVES 4

1 To make the gazpacho sauce, place the peppers, cucumber, tomato, garlic, 30ml/2 tbsp of the olive oil and the vinegar in a food processor and process until almost smooth. Season to taste with salt and ground black pepper and pack into a tub.

2 If the turkey breast steaks are quite thick, place them between two sheets of clear film and beat them with the side of a rolling pin, to flatten them slightly.

3 Spread the red pesto over the turkey, place a chorizo on each piece and roll up firmly.

4 Slice the rolls thickly and thread them on to skewers. Brush with olive oil and cook under a medium grill for about 10–12 minutes, turning once. Serve with the gazpacho sauce.

CHICKEN AND APRICOT FILO PIE

The filling for this pie has a Middle Eastern flavour – minced chicken combined with apricots, bulgur wheat, nuts and spices. It both looks and tastes spectacular.

INGREDIENTS

75g/3oz/½ cup bulgur wheat
75g/3oz/6 tbsp butter
1 onion, chopped
450g/1lb minced chicken
50g/2oz/¼ cup ready-to-eat dried apricots, finely chopped
25g/1oz/¼ cup blanched almonds, chopped
5ml/1 tsp ground cinnamon
2.5ml/½ tsp ground allspice
50ml/2fl oz/¼ cup Greek yogurt
15ml/1 tbsp snipped fresh chives, plus extra to garnish
30ml/2 tbsp chopped fresh parsley
6 large sheets filo pastry
salt and freshly ground black pepper

SERVES 6

1 Preheat the oven to 200°C/400°F/ Gas 6. Put the bulgur wheat in a large bowl with 120ml/4fl oz/½ cup boiling water. Allow the wheat to soak for 5 minutes, until the water is absorbed.

2 Heat 25g/1oz/2 tbsp of the butter in a pan and fry the onion and chicken until pale golden. Stir in the apricots, almonds and bulgur wheat and cook for a further 2 minutes. Remove from the heat and stir in the cinnamon, allspice, yogurt, chives and parsley. Season to taste with salt and pepper.

3 Melt the remaining butter. Unroll the filo pastry and cut into 25cm/10in rounds. Keep the pastry rounds covered with a clean, damp dish towel to prevent them from drying out.

4 Line a 23cm/9in loose-based flan tin with three pastry rounds, brushing each with butter as you layer them. Spoon in the chicken mixture and cover with three more pastry rounds, brushed with melted butter as before.

5 Crumple the remaining rounds and place on top of the pie. Brush with any remaining butter. Bake for 30 minutes, until golden brown and crisp. Garnish with chives and allow to cool before packing for the picnic.

CHICKEN SALAD WITH LAVENDER AND HERBS

The delightful scent of lavender has a natural affinity with sweet garlic, orange and other wild herbs. The addition of fried polenta makes this salad both filling and delicious.

INGREDIENTS

4 boneless chicken breasts
900ml/1½ pints/3¾ cups light chicken stock
175g/6oz/1 cup fine polenta or cornmeal
50g/2oz butter, plus extra for greasing
450g/1lb young spinach
175g/6oz lamb's lettuce
8 sprigs fresh lavender
8 small tomatoes, halved
salt and freshly ground black pepper

FOR THE MARINADE
6 fresh lavender flowers
10ml/2 tsp finely grated orange zest
2 garlic cloves, crushed
10ml/2 tsp clear honey
30ml/2 tbsp olive oil
10ml/2 tsp chopped fresh thyme
10ml/2 tsp chopped fresh marjoram
salt

SERVES 4

1 To make the marinade, strip the lavender flowers from the stems and combine with the orange zest, garlic, honey and salt. Add the oil and herbs. Slash the chicken deeply, spread the mixture over the chicken and leave to marinate in the fridge for 20 minutes.

2 To make the polenta, bring the chicken stock to the boil in a heavy saucepan. Add the cornmeal in a steady stream, stirring all the time until thick. Turn the cooked polenta out on to a shallow buttered tray and leave to cool.

3 Cook the chicken under the grill for 15 minutes, basting with the marinade and turning once, until cooked. Slice the chicken and let cool.

4 Cut the polenta into 2.5cm/1in cubes using a wet knife. Heat the butter in a large frying pan and fry the polenta until golden. Let cool and cut into slices before packing.

5 At the picnic site, divide the salad leaves between four plates. Arrange the chicken slices over the salad. Arrange the polenta among the salad, decorate with sprigs of lavender and tomato halves, and season with salt and freshly ground black pepper.

MARYLAND SALAD

*Succulent chicken, sweetcorn, bacon, banana and watercress combine here
in a sensational main course salad. Serve with fresh crusty bread.*

INGREDIENTS

*4 boneless chicken breasts
olive oil, for brushing
225g/8oz rindless unsmoked bacon
4 whole corn cobs
45ml/3 tbsp melted butter
4 ripe bananas, peeled and halved
4 tomatoes, halved
1 escarole or butterhead lettuce
1 bunch watercress
salt and freshly ground black
pepper*

FOR THE DRESSING
*75ml/5 tbsp groundnut oil
15ml/1 tbsp white wine vinegar
10ml/2 tsp maple syrup
10ml/2 tsp mild mustard*

SERVES 4

3 Combine the dressing ingredients with 15ml/1 tbsp water in a screw-top jar and shake well to mix. Wash and spin the lettuce leaves and pack into a box.

4 Toss the sald in the dressing and distribute between four plates. Arrange the chicken over the leaves with the bacon, banana, sweetcorn and tomatoes. Season well and serve.

1 Season the chicken breasts, brush with oil and cook under a medium grill for about 15–20 minutes, turning once. Let the chicken cool, then cut into slices. Grill the bacon for 8–10 minutes or until crisp.

2 Bring a large pan of water to the boil and cook the corn cobs for 20 minutes, until tender. Grill the bananas and tomatoes for 6–8 minutes: brush these with butter if you wish.

APRICOT DUCK WITH BEANSPROUT SALAD
∘ ∘ ∘

*Duck is rich in fat, so it stays beautifully moist when cooked under the grill,
while any excess fat drains away.*

INGREDIENTS
4 plump duck breasts, with skin
1 small red onion, thinly sliced
115g/4oz/³/4 cup ready-to-eat dried
apricots
15ml/1 tbsp clear honey
5ml/1 tsp sesame oil
10ml/2 tsp ground star anise
salt and freshly ground black
pepper

FOR THE SALAD
1/2 head Chinese leaves, finely
shredded
150g/5oz/2 cups beansprouts
2 spring onions, shredded
15ml/1 tbsp light soy sauce
15ml/1 tbsp groundnut oil
5ml/1 tsp sesame oil
5ml/1 tsp clear honey

SERVES 4

2 Tuck the slices of onion and the apricots inside the pocket and press the breast firmly back into shape. Secure with metal skewers.

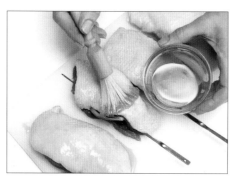

3 Mix together the clear honey and sesame oil and brush generously over the duck, particularly the skin. Sprinkle over the star anise and season with plenty of salt and black pepper.

4 To make the salad, mix together the shredded Chinese leaves, beansprouts and shredded spring onions. Pack into a box.

5 Shake together all the salad dressing ingredients in a screw-top jar. Season to taste with plenty of salt and freshly ground black pepper.

6 Cook the duck under a medium-hot grill for 12–15 minutes, turning once, until golden brown. The duck should be slightly pink in the centre.

1 Place the duck breasts, skin-side down, on a chopping board or clean work surface and cut a long slit down one side with a sharp kitchen knife, cutting not quite through, to form a large pocket.

Cook's Tip
If you prefer not to eat the beansprouts raw, they can be blanched by plunging them into boiling water for 1 minute. Drain and refresh in cold water.

FISH AND SEAFOOD

COD FILLET WITH FRESH MIXED-HERB CRUST

Use fresh herbs and wholemeal breadcrumbs to make a delicious crisp crust for the fish.
Season the fish well and serve with large lemon wedges.

INGREDIENTS

25g/1oz/2 tbsp butter
15ml/1 tbsp fresh chervil
15ml/1 tbsp fresh parsley, plus
extra sprigs to garnish
15ml/1 tbsp fresh chives
4 thick pieces of cod fillet, about
225g/8oz each, skinned
175g/6oz/3 cups breadcrumbs
15ml/1 tbsp olive oil
lemon wedges, to garnish
salt and freshly ground black
pepper

SERVES 4

1 Melt the butter and chop all the herbs finely, using a sharp knife. Brush the cod fillets with melted butter and mix any remaining butter with the breadcrumbs, fresh herbs and plenty of salt and freshly ground black pepper.

2 Press a quarter of the mixture on to each fillet, spreading evenly, and lightly sprinkle with olive oil. Grill for 10 minutes, turning once. Let the fish cool before packing. Serve the fish garnished with lemon wedges and the sprigs of fresh parsley.

MEDITERRANEAN QUICHE

This quiche forms the ideal base for a hearty picnic feast. The strong Mediterranean flavours of tomatoes, peppers and anchovies complement the cheese pastry beautifully.

INGREDIENTS

FOR THE PASTRY
225g/8oz/2 cups plain flour
pinch of salt
pinch of dry mustard
115g/4oz/½ cup butter, chilled and diced
50g/2oz Gruyère cheese, grated
salt and freshly ground black pepper

FOR THE FILLING
50g/2oz can anchovy fillets, drained
50ml/2fl oz/¼ cup milk
45ml/3 tbsp olive oil
2 large Spanish onions, peeled and sliced
1 red pepper, very finely sliced
3 egg yolks
350ml/12fl oz/1½ cups double cream
1 garlic clove, crushed
175g/6oz sharp Cheddar cheese, grated
30ml/2 tbsp French mustard
2 large tomatoes, thickly sliced
30ml/2 tbsp chopped fresh basil, to garnish

SERVES 6–8

2 Add the Gruyère cheese and process again briefly. Add enough iced water to make a stiff dough: the dough will be ready when it forms a ball. Wrap the dough in clear film and chill in the fridge for at least 30 minutes.

3 Meanwhile, make the filling. Soak the anchovies in the milk for about 20 minutes to make them less salty. Pour off the milk. Heat the olive oil in a frying pan and cook the onions and red pepper until they soften.

4 In a bowl, beat the egg yolks, cream, garlic and Cheddar cheese together; season with salt and pepper.

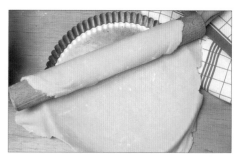

5 Preheat the oven to 200°C/400°F/ Gas 6. Roll out the chilled pastry and line a 23cm/9in loose-based quiche tin. Spread the mustard over and chill in the fridge for a further 15 minutes.

6 Arrange the tomatoes in a layer in the pastry crust. Top with the onion and pepper mixture and the anchovy fillets. Pour over the egg mixture. Bake in the oven for 30 minutes. Serve the quiche sprinkled with fresh basil.

Cook's Tip
Leave the quiche in its tin to pack it for the picnic.

1 To make the pastry, place the flour, salt and mustard in a food processor, add the butter and process the mixture until it resembles fine breadcrumbs.

SALMON STEAKS WITH OREGANO SALSA

The combination of salmon with a piquant tomato salsa works incredibly well. It is an ideal dish for an elegant picnic or summer lunch.

INGREDIENTS
15ml/1 tbsp butter
4 salmon steaks, about 225g/8oz each
120ml/4fl oz/½ cup white wine
freshly ground black pepper

FOR THE SALSA
10ml/2 tsp chopped fresh oregano, plus sprigs to garnish
4 spring onions, trimmed
225g/8oz ripe tomatoes, peeled
30ml/2 tbsp extra virgin olive oil
2.5ml/½ tsp caster sugar
15ml/1 tbsp tomato purée

SERVES 4

1 Butter four squares of double-thickness baking foil. Put a salmon steak on each and add a little wine and a grinding of ground black pepper. Wrap the salmon steaks loosely in the squares, sealing the edges securely. Cook under a medium-hot grill for 10 minutes. Allow the steaks to cool before packing into a box.

2 Put the chopped fresh oregano in a food processor and chop it very finely. Add the spring onions, tomatoes and remaining salsa ingredients. Pulse until chopped but not a smooth purée. Pack into an airtight container.

3 Serve the salmon with the salsa, garnished with a sprig of fresh oregano.

Salmon with Red Onion Marmalade

° ° °

Salmon grills well but is most successful when it is at least 2.5cm/1in thick. The red onion marmalade is rich and delicious. Puréed blackcurrants work as well as crème de cassis.

INGREDIENTS
30ml/2 tbsp olive oil
4 salmon steaks, about 175g/6oz each
salt and freshly ground black pepper

FOR THE RED ONION MARMALADE
50g/2oz/4 tbsp butter
5 medium red onions, peeled and finely sliced
175ml/6floz/³⁄4 cup red wine vinegar
50ml/2fl oz/¹⁄4 cup crème de cassis
50ml/2fl oz/¹⁄4 cup grenadine
50ml/2fl oz/¹⁄4 cup red wine

SERVES 4

1 Use your hands to rub the olive oil into the salmon flesh and season well with plenty of salt and freshly ground black pepper.

2 Melt the butter in a large heavy-based saucepan and add the sliced onions. Sauté the onions for 5 minutes until golden brown.

3 Stir in the vinegar, crème de cassis, grenadine and wine and continue to cook for about 10 minutes until the liquid has almost entirely evaporated and the onions are glazed. Season well.

4 Brush the fish with a little more oil, and cook under the grill for about 6–8 minutes, turning once.

SALMON WITH TROPICAL FRUIT SALSA

*Fresh salmon needs little adornment, but it combines very well
with the exotic flavours in this colourful salsa for an elegant picnic meal.*

INGREDIENTS

4 salmon steaks or fillets, about
175g/6oz each
finely grated rind and juice of
1 lime
1 small, ripe mango
1 small, ripe pawpaw
1 red chilli
45ml/3 tbsp chopped fresh
coriander
salt and freshly ground black
pepper

SERVES 4

1 Place the salmon in a wide dish and sprinkle over half the lime rind and juice. Season with salt and pepper.

2 Cut the mango in half, cutting either side of the stone, and remove the stone. Finely chop the mango flesh and place the chunks in a bowl.

3 Halve the pawpaw, scoop out the seeds with a spoon and remove the peel. Finely chop the flesh and add it to the mango chunks in the bowl.

4 Cut the chilli in half lengthways. Leave the seeds in to make the salsa hot and spicy, or remove them for a milder flavour. Finely chop the chilli.

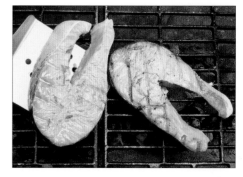

5 Combine the mango, pawpaw, chilli and coriander in a bowl and stir in the remaining lime rind and juice. Season with salt and black pepper and pack into a box.

6 Cook the salmon under the grill for about 5–8 minutes, turning once. Serve with the fruit salsa.

SWORDFISH KEBABS

Swordfish has a firm meaty texture that makes it ideal for kebabs.
Marinade the fish first to keep it moist.

INGREDIENTS

900g/2lb swordfish steaks
45ml/3 tbsp olive oil
juice of ½ lemon
1 garlic clove, crushed
5ml/1 tsp paprika
3 tomatoes, quartered
2 onions, cut into wedges
salt and freshly ground black pepper
salad and pitta bread, to serve

SERVES 4–6

1 Use a large kitchen knife to cut the swordfish steaks into large cubes. Arrange the cubes in a single layer in a large shallow dish.

2 Blend together the olive oil, lemon juice, garlic, paprika and seasoning in a bowl, and pour over the fish. Cover the dish loosely with clear film and leave to marinate in a cool place for up to 2 hours.

3 Thread the fish cubes on to metal skewers, alternating them with the pieces of tomato and onion wedges.

4 Cook the kebabs under a hot grill for about 5–10 minutes, basting frequently with the remaining marinade and turning occasionally. Serve with salad and pitta bread.

SMOKED MACKEREL WITH BLUEBERRIES

Fresh blueberries burst with flavour when cooked, and their sharpness complements the rich flesh of mackerel very well.

INGREDIENTS

15g/¹⁄₂oz plain flour
4 smoked mackerel fillets
50g/2oz/4 tbsp unsalted butter
juice of ¹⁄₂ lemon
salt and freshly ground black
pepper

FOR THE BLUEBERRY SAUCE
450g/1lb blueberries
25g/1oz/2 tbsp caster sugar
15g/¹⁄₂oz/1 tbsp unsalted butter
salt and freshly ground black
pepper

SERVES 4

1 Preheat the oven to 200°C/400°F/ Gas 6. Season the flour with salt and pepper. Coat each fish fillet in the flour.

2 Brush the fillets with butter and bake in the oven for 20 minutes. Allow to cool before packing.

3 To make the sauce, place the blueberries, sugar, butter and salt and pepper in a small roasting pan and cook for 10 minutes. Pack the sauce separately. At the picnic site, drizzle the lemon juice over the mackerel and serve with the blueberries on the side.

Vegetarian
and Vegetable
Dishes

GRILLED VEGETABLE TERRINE

A colourful, layered terrine, using all the vegetables associated with the Mediterranean, makes a successful and elegant dish for outdoor eating. Barbecuing the vegetables would add to the flavour.

INGREDIENTS

2 large red peppers, quartered, cored and seeded
2 large yellow peppers, quartered, cored and seeded
1 large aubergine, sliced lengthways
2 large courgettes, sliced lengthways
90ml/6 tbsp olive oil
1 large red onion, thinly sliced
75g/3oz/1/2 cup raisins
15ml/1 tbsp tomato purée
15ml/1 tbsp red wine vinegar
400ml/14fl oz/1²/3 cups tomato juice
15g/1/2oz/2 tbsp powdered gelatine
fresh basil leaves, to garnish

FOR THE DRESSING
90ml/6 tbsp extra virgin olive oil
30ml/2 tbsp red wine vinegar
salt and freshly ground black pepper

SERVES 6

1 Grill the peppers, skin-side down, on a hot barbecue or grill, until the skins are beginning to blacken. Transfer to a bowl, cover and leave to cool.

2 Brush the aubergine and courgette slices with oil and cook until tender and golden, turning occasionally.

3 Heat the remaining oil in a pan and add the onion, raisins, tomato purée and red wine vinegar. Cook until soft and syrupy. Leave to cool in the pan.

4 Pour half the tomato juice into a saucepan and sprinkle with the gelatine. Dissolve gently over a very low heat, stirring continuously.

5 Line an oiled 1.75 litre/3 pint/ 7½ cup terrine with clear film, leaving a little hanging over the sides. Place a layer of red peppers in the bottom and pour in enough of the tomato juice with gelatine to cover. Repeat with the aubergines, courgettes, yellow peppers and onion mixture, ending with another layer of red peppers and covering each layer with tomato juice and gelatine.

6 Add the remaining tomato juice to any left in the pan and pour into the terrine. Give it a sharp tap to eliminate air bubbles. Cover the terrine with clear film and chill until set.

7 To make the dressing, whisk the oil and vinegar, and season with salt and black pepper. Turn out the terrine and serve in thick slices, drizzled with the dressing. Garnish with the basil leaves.

TOFU SATAY

Grill cubes of tofu until crispy then serve with a Thai-style peanut sauce for a simple but interesting picnic meal.

INGREDIENTS
2 × 200g/7oz packs smoked tofu
45ml/3 tbsp light soy sauce
10ml/2 tsp sesame oil
1 garlic clove, crushed
1 yellow and 1 red pepper, cut in squares
8–12 fresh bay leaves
sunflower oil, for brushing

FOR THE PEANUT SAUCE
2 spring onions, finely chopped
2 garlic cloves, crushed
good pinch chilli powder, or a few drops hot chilli sauce
5ml/1 tsp sugar
15ml/1 tbsp white wine vinegar
30ml/2 tbsp light soy sauce
45ml/3 tbsp crunchy peanut butter

SERVES 4–6

1 Cut the tofu into bite-sized cubes and place in a large bowl. Add the soy sauce, sesame oil and crushed garlic and mix well. Cover with clear film and marinate for at least 20 minutes.

2 Beat all the peanut sauce ingredients together in a large bowl, using a wooden spoon, until well blended. Avoid using a food processor to blend the ingredients, as the texture should be slightly chunky.

3 Drain the tofu and thread the cubes on to 8–12 satay sticks, alternating the tofu with the pepper squares and bay leaves. Larger bay leaves may need to be halved before threading.

4 Brush the satays with sunflower oil and grill, turning the sticks occasionally, until the tofu and peppers are browned and crisp. Serve with the peanut sauce.

CASSAVA AND VEGETABLE KEBABS

This is an attractive and delicious assortment of African vegetables, marinated in a spicy garlic sauce, then roasted over hot coals. If cassava is unavailable, use sweet potato or yam instead.

INGREDIENTS

175g/6oz cassava
1 onion, cut into wedges
1 aubergine, cut into bite-sized pieces
1 courgette, sliced
1 ripe plantain, sliced
½ red pepper and ½ green pepper, sliced
16 cherry tomatoes
rice or couscous, to serve

FOR THE MARINADE
60ml/4 tbsp lemon juice
60ml/4 tbsp olive oil
45–60ml/3–4 tbsp soy sauce
15ml/1 tbsp tomato paste
1 green chilli, seeded and finely chopped
½ onion, grated
2 garlic cloves, crushed
5ml/1 tsp mixed spice
pinch of dried thyme

SERVES 4

1 Peel the cassava and cut into bite-sized pieces. Place in a large bowl, cover with boiling water and leave to blanch for about 5 minutes. Drain well.

2 Place all the prepared vegetables, including the cassava, in a large bowl and mix with your hands so that all the vegetables are evenly distributed.

3 Blend the marinade ingredients in a jug and pour over the vegetables. Cover and leave to marinate for 1–2 hours.

4 Thread the vegetables, with the cherry tomatoes, on to eight skewers and grill for about 15 minutes until tender and browned. Turn the skewers frequently and baste them occasionally with the marinade.

5 Meanwhile, pour the remaining marinade into a small saucepan and simmer for about 10 minutes to reduce. Strain the reduced marinade into a jug. Serve the kebabs on a bed of rice or couscous, with the sauce on the side.

RED BEAN AND MUSHROOM BURGERS

· · ·

Vegetarians, vegans and meat-eaters alike will enjoy these healthy, low-fat veggie burgers.
With salad, pitta bread and Greek-style yogurt, they make a substantial picnic meal.

INGREDIENTS

15ml/1 tbsp olive oil
1 small onion, finely chopped
1 garlic clove, crushed
5ml/1 tsp ground cumin
5ml/1 tsp ground coriander
2.5ml/½ tsp ground turmeric
115g/4oz/1½ cups finely chopped
mushrooms
400g/14oz can red kidney beans
30ml/2 tbsp chopped fresh
coriander
wholemeal flour (optional)
olive oil, for brushing
salt and freshly ground black
pepper
Greek-style yogurt, to serve

SERVES 4

1 Heat the olive oil in a frying pan and fry the chopped onion and garlic over a moderate heat, stirring, until softened. Add the spices and cook for a further minute, stirring continuously.

Cook's Tip

These burgers are not quite as firm as meat burgers, and will need careful handling on the barbecue.

2 Add the chopped mushrooms and cook, stirring, until softened and dry. Remove the pan from the heat and empty the contents into a large bowl.

3 Drain the beans thoroughly, place them in a bowl and mash with a fork.

4 Stir the kidney beans into the frying pan, with the chopped fresh coriander, and mix thoroughly. Season the mixture well with plenty of salt and freshly ground black pepper.

5 Using floured hands, form the mixture into four flat burger shapes. If the mixture is too sticky to handle, mix in a little wholemeal flour.

6 Lightly brush the burgers with olive oil and grill for 8–10 minutes, turning once, until golden brown. Serve with a spoonful of yogurt and a green salad, if liked.

LOOFAH AND AUBERGINE RATATOUILLE
∘ ∘ ∘

Loofahs are edible gourds with spongy, creamy-white flesh. Like aubergine, their flavour is intensified by roasting. Serve with plenty of crusty French bread.

INGREDIENTS

1 large or 2 medium aubergines
450g/1lb young loofahs or sponge gourds
1 large red pepper, cut into large chunks
225g/8oz cherry tomatoes
225g/8oz shallots
10ml/2 tsp ground coriander
60ml/4 tbsp olive oil
2 garlic cloves, finely chopped
a few fresh coriander sprigs
salt and freshly ground black pepper

SERVES 4

1 Cut the aubergines into thick chunks and sprinkle the pieces liberally with salt to draw out the bitter juices. Leave to drain for about 45 minutes, then rinse under cold running water and pat dry with kitchen paper.

2 Preheat the oven to 200°C/400°F/ Gas 6. Slice the loofahs into 2cm/³⁄₄in pieces. Place the aubergines, loofah and pepper pieces, together with the cherry tomatoes and shallots, in a roasting pan large enough to take all the vegetables in a single layer.

3 Sprinkle the vegetables with the ground coriander and olive oil. Scatter the chopped garlic and fresh coriander leaves on top and season to taste.

4 Cook in the oven for about 25 minutes, stirring the vegetables occasionally, until the loofah is golden and the peppers are beginning to char. As an alternative, you could thread the vegetables on skewers and grill them.

WILD RICE WITH VEGETABLES

Wild rice makes a special accompaniment to roasted vegetables in a simple vinaigrette dressing. This recipe can be served as a side dish, but it also makes a tasty meal on its own.

INGREDIENTS

225g/8oz/1 cup wild and long grain
rice mixture
1 large aubergine, thickly sliced
1 red, 1 yellow and 1 green pepper,
quartered, cored and seeded
2 red onions, sliced
225g/8oz shiitake mushrooms
2 small courgettes, cut in half
lengthways
olive oil, for brushing
30ml/2 tbsp chopped fresh thyme

FOR THE DRESSING
90ml/6 tbsp extra virgin olive oil
30ml/2 tbsp balsamic vinegar
2 garlic cloves, crushed
salt and freshly ground black
pepper

SERVES 4

1 Put the wild and long grain rice mixture in a pan of cold salted water. Bring to the boil, then reduce the heat, cover and cook gently for about 30–40 minutes until the grains are tender (or follow the cooking instructions on the packet, if appropriate). Drain.

2 To make the dressing, mix together the olive oil, vinegar, crushed garlic and salt and pepper in a screw-top jar until well blended.

3 Arrange the vegetables on a rack. Brush with olive oil and grill for about 8–10 minutes, until tender and well browned, turning them occasionally and basting with oil.

4 At the picnic site, toss half the dressing in with the rice and arrange the vegetables on top. Pour over the remaining dressing and scatter over the chopped fresh thyme.

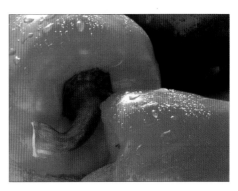

STUFFED TOMATOES AND PEPPERS

Colourful peppers and tomatoes make perfect containers for meat and vegetable stuffings. The flavours in this dish are simply superb.

INGREDIENTS

2 large ripe tomatoes
1 green pepper
1 yellow or orange pepper
60ml/4 tbsp olive oil, plus extra for sprinkling
2 onions, chopped
2 garlic cloves, crushed
50g/2oz/½ cup blanched almonds, chopped
75g/3oz/scant ½ cup long grain rice, boiled and drained
30ml/2 tbsp fresh mint, roughly chopped
30ml/2 tbsp fresh parsley, roughly chopped
25g/1oz/2 tbsp sultanas
45ml/3 tbsp ground almonds
salt and freshly ground black pepper
chopped mixed fresh herbs, to garnish

SERVES 4

2 Halve the peppers, leaving the cores intact. Scoop out the seeds. Brush the peppers with 15ml/1 tbsp olive oil and grill for 15 minutes. Place the peppers and tomatoes on a grill rack and season well with salt and freshly ground black pepper.

3 Fry the onions in the remaining olive oil for 5 minutes. Add the crushed garlic and chopped almonds to the pan and fry for a further minute.

4 Remove the pan from the heat and stir in the rice, chopped tomatoes, mint, parsley and sultanas. Season well with salt and pepper and spoon the mixture into the tomatoes and peppers.

1 Cut the tomatoes in half and scoop out the pulp and seeds, using a teaspoon. Leave the tomatoes to drain on kitchen paper with the cut sides facing down. Roughly chop the tomato pulp and set it aside.

5 Scatter with the ground almonds and sprinkle with a little extra olive oil. Grill for about 15 minutes. Garnish with fresh herbs.

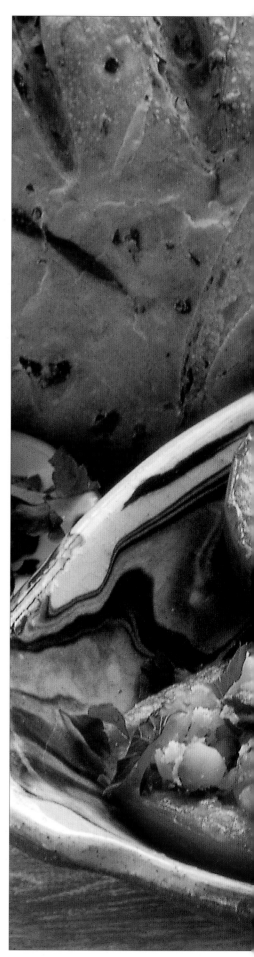

COUSCOUS-STUFFED PEPPERS

Couscous makes a good basis for a stuffing, and in this recipe it is studded with raisins and flavoured with fresh mint. Charred peppers make the combination of flavours truly special.

2 To cook the couscous, bring 250ml/8fl oz/1 cup water to the boil. Add the oil and salt, then remove from the heat and add the couscous. Stir and leave to stand, covered, for 5 minutes. Stir in the onion, raisins and mint. Season well and stir in the egg yolk.

3 Use a teaspoon to fill the peppers with the couscous mixture to about three-quarters full (the couscous will swell while cooking). Wrap each pepper in a piece of oiled baking foil.

4 Grill the peppers for 20 minutes, until tender. Serve at the picnic site garnished with fresh mint leaves.

INGREDIENTS

6 peppers
25g/1oz/2 tbsp butter
1 onion, finely chopped
5ml/1 tsp olive oil
2.5ml/½ tsp salt
175g/6oz/1 cup couscous
25g/1oz/2 tbsp raisins
30ml/2 tbsp chopped fresh mint
1 egg yolk
salt and freshly ground black
pepper
mint leaves, to garnish

SERVES 4

1 Carefully slit each pepper with a sharp knife and remove the core and seeds. Melt the butter in a small saucepan and add the chopped onion. Cook until soft but not browned.

SPANISH POTATOES

This is an adaptation of a traditional recipe for peppery fried potatoes. Cook the potatoes in a pan on the hob, and serve them with any meat or vegetable dish.

INGREDIENTS

675g/1½ lb small new potatoes
75ml/5 tbsp olive oil
2 garlic cloves, sliced
2.5ml/½ tsp crushed chillies
2.5ml/½ tsp ground cumin
10ml/2 tsp paprika
30ml/2 tbsp red or white wine vinegar
1 red or green pepper, sliced
coarse sea salt, to serve (optional)

SERVES 4

1 Cook the potatoes in a saucepan of boiling salted water until almost tender. Drain and cut into chunks.

2 Heat the olive oil in a large frying pan or sauté pan and fry the potatoes, turning them frequently, until golden.

3 Meanwhile, crush together the garlic, chillies and cumin using a pestle and mortar. Mix with the paprika and wine vinegar to form a thick paste.

4 Add the garlic mixture to the potatoes with the sliced pepper and cook, stirring, for 2 minutes. Leave until cold. Scatter with coarse sea salt, if you wish, to serve.

SALADS AND
ACCOMPANIMENTS

TOMATO AND FETA CHEESE SALAD

Sweet sun-ripened tomatoes are rarely more delicious than when mixed with feta cheese and olive oil. This salad can be served with any barbecued meats, fish or vegetables.

INGREDIENTS

900g/2lb tomatoes
200g/7oz feta cheese
120ml/4fl oz/½ cup olive oil
12 black olives
4 sprigs fresh basil
freshly ground black pepper

SERVES 4

3 Crumble the feta cheese over the tomatoes, sprinkle with olive oil, then sprinkle with olives and fresh basil. Season with freshly ground black pepper and pack into a box.

1 Remove the tough cores from the tomatoes with a small kitchen knife.

2 Slice the tomatoes thickly on a chopping board and arrange the slices in a wide-based shallow dish.

Cook's Tip

Feta cheese has a strong flavour and can be very salty. For an authentic flavour and texture, look out for Greek, Cypriot or Turkish feta.

GREEN BEAN SALAD WITH EGG TOPPING

When green beans are fresh and plentiful, serve them lightly cooked as a salad topped with butter-fried breadcrumbs, egg and fresh parsley.

INGREDIENTS

675g/1½ lb green beans, topped and tailed
30ml/2 tbsp extra virgin olive oil
30ml/2 tbsp butter
50g/2oz/1 cup fresh white breadcrumbs
60ml/4 tbsp chopped fresh parsley
1 egg, hard-boiled and shelled
salt

SERVES 4

1 Bring a large pan of salted water to the boil. Add the beans and cook for 6 minutes. Drain well, toss the beans in olive oil and allow to cool.

2 Heat the butter in a large frying pan, add the breadcrumbs and fry until golden. Remove the frying pan from the heat, add the chopped fresh parsley, then grate in the hard-boiled egg.

3 Place the beans in a shallow box and spoon on the breadcrumb topping. The salad can be prepared in advance and chilled in the fridge until needed.

POTATO SALAD WITH SAUSAGE

The addition of garlic sausage makes this a substantial salad to serve as part of a picnic, but if it is to accompany meat or fish you can make it with potatoes alone.

INGREDIENTS
450g/1lb small waxy potatoes
30–45ml/2–3 tbsp dry white wine
2 shallots, finely chopped
15ml/1 tbsp chopped fresh parsley
15ml/1 tbsp chopped fresh tarragon
175g/6oz French garlic sausage
fresh parsley, to garnish
salt and freshly ground black pepper

FOR THE VINAIGRETTE
10ml/2 tsp Dijon mustard
15ml/1 tbsp tarragon vinegar or white wine vinegar
75ml/5 tbsp extra virgin olive oil

SERVES 4

1 Cook the potatoes in boiling salted water for 10–15 minutes, until tender. Drain them, and refresh under cold running water. Cut them into 5mm/ ¼ in slices, place them in a large bowl and sprinkle with the white wine and the chopped shallots.

2 To make the vinaigrette, mix the Dijon mustard and vinegar in a small bowl, then whisk in the olive oil, 15ml/1 tbsp at a time. Season well with salt and freshly ground black pepper and pour over the potatoes.

3 Add the chopped fresh parsley and tarragon to the potatoes in the bowl and toss until well mixed.

4 Slice the garlic sausage thinly and toss with the potatoes. Season with salt and pepper to taste and pack into a box, garnished with parsley.

TABBOULEH
◦ ◦ ◦

*This classic Lebanese salad has become very popular everywhere. It makes an ideal substitute
for a rice dish and is especially good with roasted meat.*

INGREDIENTS
*175g/6oz/1 cup fine bulgur wheat
juice of 1 lemon
45ml/3 tbsp olive oil
40g/1½ oz fresh parsley, finely
chopped
45ml/3 tbsp fresh mint, chopped
4–5 spring onions, chopped
1 green pepper, sliced
salt and freshly ground black
pepper
2 large tomatoes, diced, and black
olives, to garnish*

SERVES 4

1 Put the bulgur wheat in a large
bowl. Add enough cold water to cover
the wheat and let it stand for at least
30 minutes and up to 2 hours.

2 Drain and squeeze the wheat
with your hands to remove excess
water. The bulgur wheat will swell
to double its original size. Spread
the wheat on kitchen paper to allow
to dry completely.

3 Place the bulgur wheat in a large
bowl, add the lemon juice, the olive oil
and a little salt and pepper. Allow to
stand for 1–2 hours if possible, in
order for the flavours to develop.

4 Add the chopped parsley, mint,
spring onions and pepper to the wheat
in the bowl and mix well. Garnish with
diced tomatoes and olives. The
tabbouleh can be prepared in advance,
covered with clear film and stored in
the fridge until needed.

GRILLED HALLOUMI AND GRAPE SALAD

∘ ∘ ∘

In the eastern Mediterranean, halloumi cheese is often served grilled or fried for breakfast or supper. In this recipe it's tossed with sweet, juicy grapes that complement its distinctive flavour.

INGREDIENTS

150g/5oz mixed green salad leaves
75g/3oz seedless green grapes
75g/3oz seedless black grapes
250g/9oz halloumi cheese
30ml/2 tbsp olive oil
fresh young thyme leaves or dill,
to garnish

FOR THE DRESSING
60ml/4 tbsp olive oil
15ml/1 tbsp lemon juice
2.5ml/½ tsp caster sugar
15ml/1 tbsp chopped fresh thyme
or dill
salt and freshly ground black
pepper

SERVES 4

1 To make the dressing, mix the olive oil, lemon juice and sugar together in a bowl. Season well with plenty of salt and black pepper. Stir in the chopped fresh thyme or dill and pour into a screw-top jar for transporting to the picnic site.

2 Toss together the mixed green salad leaves and the green and black grapes, then transfer to a box or tub.

3 Slice the halloumi cheese. Brush the slices with olive oil and pan-fry briefly until golden, turning once.

4 Arrange the cooked cheese over the salad. Pour over the dressing and garnish with thyme or dill leaves.

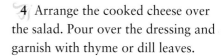

APPLE COLESLAW

There are many variations of this traditional salad; this recipe combines the sweet flavours of apple and carrot with a hint of celery. Prepare the salad in advance and chill until needed.

INGREDIENTS
450g/1lb white cabbage
1 medium onion
2 apples, peeled and cored
175g/6oz carrots, peeled
150ml/¼ pint/²/₃ cup mayonnaise
5ml/1 tsp celery salt
freshly ground black pepper

SERVES 4

1 Remove the outer leaves from the white cabbage and, using a heavy knife, cut it into 5cm/2in wedges. Remove and discard the stem sections.

2 Feed the cabbage wedges and the onion through the slicing blade of a food processor. Change to a grating blade and grate the apples and carrots. If you do not have a food processor, use a vegetable slicer and a hand grater.

3 Combine the salad ingredients in a large mixing bowl. Fold in the mayonnaise and season with celery salt and freshly ground black pepper.

Cook's Tip
This recipe can be adapted easily to suit different tastes. Add 115g/4oz/½ cup chopped walnuts or raisins for added texture, or, for a richer, more substantial coleslaw, add 115g/4oz/½ cup grated Cheddar cheese.

MELLOW GARLIC DIP
∘ ∘ ∘

Two whole heads of garlic may seem too much but, once cooked, the taste is sweet and mellow.
Serve with crunchy bread sticks and potato crisps.

2 When cool enough to handle, separate the garlic cloves and peel. Place on a chopping board and sprinkle with salt. Mash the garlic with a fork until puréed.

3 Place the garlic in a large bowl and stir in the mayonnaise, yogurt and wholegrain mustard. Mix well.

4 Check the seasoning, adding more salt and pepper to taste, then spoon the dip into a tub. Cover and chill in the fridge until needed.

INGREDIENTS
2 whole garlic heads
15ml/1 tbsp olive oil
60ml/4 tbsp mayonnaise
75ml/5 tbsp Greek-style yogurt
5ml/1 tsp wholegrain mustard
salt and freshly ground black pepper

SERVES 4

1 Slice the tops from the heads of garlic, using a sharp knife. Brush with olive oil and place in a roasting tin. Cook in the oven for 25 minutes, turning occasionally.

GUACAMOLE

Nachos or tortilla chips are the classic accompaniments for this Mexican dip, but it also tastes great served on the side with sandwiches or salads.

INGREDIENTS

2 ripe avocados
2 red chillies, seeded
1 garlic clove
1 shallot
30ml/2 tbsp olive oil, plus
extra to serve
juice of 1 lemon
salt
fresh flat leaf parsley, to garnish

SERVES 4

1 Halve the avocados, flick out the stones, using the point of a sharp knife, and use a dessert spoon to scoop the flesh into a large bowl.

2 Mash the flesh well, using a potato masher or a large fork, so that the avocado is a fairly smooth consistency.

3 Finely chop the chillies, garlic clove and shallot, then stir into the mashed avocado with the olive oil and lemon juice. Add salt to taste and mix well.

4 Spoon the mixture into a serving bowl. Drizzle over a little more olive oil and scatter with flat leaf parsley leaves. Guacamole will not keep for very long but can be prepared up to 8 hours in advance and stored in the fridge, sprinkled with lemon juice and covered with clear film.

CREAMY AUBERGINE DIP

. . .

*Spread this velvet-textured dip thickly on to slices of French bread toasted under the grill,
then top with slivers of sun-dried tomato to make wonderful Italian-style crostini.*

INGREDIENTS

1 large aubergine
30ml/2 tbsp olive oil
1 small onion, finely chopped
2 garlic cloves, finely chopped
60ml/4 tbsp chopped fresh parsley
75ml/5 tbsp crème fraîche
red Tabasco sauce, to taste
juice of 1 lemon, to taste
salt and freshly ground black
pepper

SERVES 4

3 Peel the aubergine and mash the flesh with a large fork or potato masher to make a pulpy purée.

4 Stir in the onion and garlic, parsley and crème fraîche. Add Tabasco, lemon juice, and season to taste.

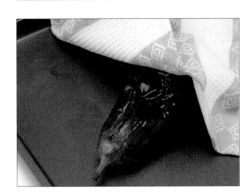

1 Cook the whole aubergine under a medium grill for about 20 minutes, turning occasionally, until the skin is blackened and the aubergine soft. Cover the aubergine with a clean dish towel and set aside to cool for about 5–6 minutes.

2 Heat the oil in a frying pan and cook the chopped onion and garlic for 5 minutes, until soft but not browned.

Outdoor Entertaining

GRILLED ASPARAGUS WITH SALT-CURED HAM

Grilled or barbecued asparagus has a wonderfully intense flavour that stands up well to the wrapping of crisp, salty ham. Serve this traditional tapas dish with apéritifs before a meal.

INGREDIENTS

6 slices of Serrano ham

12 asparagus spears

15ml/1 tbsp olive oil

sea salt and coarsely ground black pepper

SERVES 4

1 Halve each slice of ham lengthways and wrap one half around each of the asparagus spears.

2 Brush the ham and asparagus lightly with olive oil and sprinkle with salt and pepper. Cook under the grill or on the barbecue for about 4 minutes, turning frequently, until the asparagus is tender but still firm. Serve at once.

Cook's Tip

If you can't find Serrano ham, try using Italian prosciutto or Portuguese presunto.

SALMON WITH SPICY PESTO

This is a great way to bone salmon steaks to give a solid piece of fish. The pesto uses sunflower kernels and chilli as its flavouring, rather than the classic basil and pine nuts.

INGREDIENTS

4 salmon steaks, about
225g/8oz each
30ml/2 tbsp sunflower oil
finely grated rind and juice
of 1 lime
salt and freshly ground
black pepper

FOR THE PESTO
6 mild fresh red chillies
2 garlic cloves
30ml/2 tbsp sunflower or
pumpkin seeds
juice and finely grated rind
of 1 lime
75ml/5 tbsp olive oil

SERVES 4

1 Insert a very sharp knife close to the top of the bone. Working closely to the bone, cut your way to the end of the steak to release one side. Repeat with the other side. Pull out any extra visible bones with a pair of tweezers.

2 Sprinkle salt on the work surface and take hold of the end of the salmon piece, skin-side down. Insert the knife between the skin and the flesh and, working away from you, remove the skin, keeping the knife as close to it as possible. Repeat for each piece of fish.

3 Curl each piece of fish into a round, with the thinner end wrapped around the fatter end. Secure the shape tightly with a length of string.

4 Rub the sunflower oil into the boneless fish rounds. Put the salmon into a large bowl or dish and add the lime juice and rind and the salt and pepper. Allow the salmon to marinate in the fridge for up to 2 hours.

5 For the pesto, de-seed the chillies and place with the garlic cloves, sunflower or pumpkin seeds, lime juice, rind and seasoning in a food processor. Process until well mixed. Pour the olive oil gradually over the moving blades until the sauce has thickened and emulsified. Drain the salmon from its marinade. Cook the fish steaks under the grill for 5 minutes each side and serve with the spicy pesto.

TOMATO AND CHEESE TARTS

These crisp little tartlets look impressive but are actually very easy to make.
They are best eaten fresh from the oven.

INGREDIENTS

3 sheets filo pastry
1 egg white
175g/6oz cream cheese
handful fresh basil leaves
4 small tomatoes, sliced
salt and freshly ground black
pepper

MAKES 12

1 Preheat the oven to 200°C/400°F/
Gas 6. Brush the sheets of filo pastry
lightly with egg white and cut into
24 × 10cm/4in squares.

2 Layer the squares in twos, in
12 bun tins. Spoon the cream cheese
into the pastry cases. Season with
ground black pepper and top with
fresh basil leaves.

3 Arrange the tomatoes on the tarts,
season and bake for 10–12 minutes,
until the pastry is golden. Serve warm.

Cook's Tip
Use halved cherry tomatoes
for the tarts, if you prefer.

GRILLED MUSSELS WITH PARSLEY AND PARMESAN

For a barbecue party, mussels make an ideal dish: the irresistible aroma as they cook means that they will be devoured the moment they are ready.

INGREDIENTS

450g/1lb fresh mussels
45ml/3 tbsp water
15ml/1 tbsp melted butter
15ml/1 tbsp olive oil
45ml/3 tbsp freshly grated
Parmesan cheese
30ml/2 tbsp chopped fresh parsley
2 garlic cloves, finely chopped
2.5ml/½ tsp coarsely ground black
pepper

SERVES 4

2 Place the mussels with the water in a large saucepan. Cover with the lid and steam for 5 minutes, or until all of the mussels have opened.

4 In a large bowl, mix together the melted butter, olive oil, grated Parmesan cheese, chopped parsley, garlic and ground black pepper.

1 Scrub the mussels, scraping off any barnacles and pulling out the beards. Tap any closed mussels sharply with a knife and discard any that fail to open.

3 Drain the mussels, discarding any that remain closed. Snap the top shell off each, leaving the mussel still attached to the bottom shell.

5 Using a spoon, place a small amount of the cheese mixture on top of each mussel.

6 Cook the mussels in a saucepan on a medium barbecue for 2–3 minutes or until the mussels are sizzling hot. Serve immediately, with crusty French bread.

GRILLED KING PRAWNS WITH ROMESCO SAUCE

° ° °

This sauce comes from the Catalan region of Spain and is served with fish and seafood.
Its main ingredients are sweet pepper, tomatoes, garlic and almonds.

INGREDIENTS

24 uncooked king prawns
30–45ml/2–3 tbsp olive oil
flat leaf parsley, to garnish
lemon wedges, to serve

FOR THE SAUCE

2 well-flavoured tomatoes
60ml/4 tbsp olive oil
1 onion, chopped
4 garlic cloves, chopped
1 canned pimiento, chopped
2.5ml/½ tsp dried chilli flakes or
powder
75ml/5 tbsp fish stock
30ml/2 tbsp white wine
10 blanched almonds
15ml/1 tbsp red wine vinegar
salt

SERVES 4

1 To make the sauce, immerse the tomatoes in boiling water for about 30 seconds, then refresh them under cold running water. Peel away the skins and roughly chop the flesh.

2 Heat 30ml/2 tbsp of the oil. Add the onion and three of the garlic cloves and cook until soft. Add the pimiento, tomatoes, chilli, fish stock and wine. Cover and simmer for 30 minutes.

3 Toast the almonds under the grill until golden. Transfer to a blender or food processor and grind coarsely. Add the remaining 30ml/2 tbsp of oil, the vinegar and the last garlic clove and process until evenly combined. Add the tomato and pimiento sauce and process until smooth. Season with salt.

4 Remove the heads from the prawns, leaving them otherwise unshelled and, with a sharp knife, slit each one down the back and remove the dark vein. Rinse and pat dry on kitchen paper. Toss the prawns in olive oil, then spread them out on the grill rack or barbecue and cook for about 2–3 minutes on each side, until pink. Serve at once, garnished with parsley and accompanied by lemon wedges and the romesco sauce.

SIRLOIN STEAKS WITH BLOODY MARY SAUCE

*This cocktail of ingredients is just as delicious as the drink that inspired it, and as the alcohol
evaporates in cooking, you need not worry about a hangover.*

INGREDIENTS

*4 sirloin steaks, about
225g/8oz each*

FOR THE MARINADE
*30ml/2 tbsp dark soy sauce
60ml/4 tbsp balsamic vinegar
30ml/2 tbsp olive oil*

FOR THE BLOODY MARY SAUCE
*1kg/2¼lb very ripe tomatoes,
peeled and chopped
tomato purée, if required
50g/2oz/½ cup chopped onions
2 spring onions
5ml/1 tsp chopped fresh coriander
5ml/1 tsp ground cumin
5ml/1 tsp salt
15ml/1 tbsp fresh lime juice
120ml/4fl oz/½ cup beef
consommé
60ml/4 tbsp vodka
15ml/1 tbsp Worcestershire sauce*

SERVES 4

1 Lay the steaks in a shallow dish.
Mix the marinade ingredients together,
pour over the steaks and leave to
marinate in the fridge for at least
2 hours, turning once or twice.

2 Place all the sauce ingredients in
a food processor and blend to a fairly
smooth texture. If the tomatoes are
not quite ripe, add a little tomato
purée. Put in a saucepan, bring to the
boil and simmer for about 5 minutes.

3 Remove the steaks from the dish
and discard the marinade. Cook the
steaks on a medium-hot barbecue
for about 3–6 minutes each side,
depending on how rare you like them,
turning once during cooking. Serve the
steaks with the Bloody Mary sauce.

PEPPER STEAK

This easy, rather indulgent bistro classic can be put together in a matter of minutes for an intimate summer supper in the garden. The creamy sauce helps to balance the heat of the pepper.

INGREDIENTS

30ml/2 tbsp black peppercorns
2 fillet or sirloin steaks, about
225g/8oz each
15g/½ oz/1 tbsp butter
10ml/2 tsp olive oil
45ml/3 tbsp brandy
150ml/¼ pint/⅔ cup whipping
cream
1 garlic clove, finely chopped
salt, if necessary

SERVES 2

1 Place the black peppercorns in a sturdy polythene bag. Crush the peppercorns with a rolling pin or steak hammer until they are crushed to medium-coarse pepper.

2 Put the steaks on a chopping board and trim away any excess fat, using a sharp kitchen knife. Press the pepper firmly on to both sides of the meat, to coat it completely.

3 Melt the butter with the olive oil in a heavy frying pan over a medium-high heat. Add the meat and cook for 6–7 minutes, turning once, until cooked to your liking. Transfer the steaks to a warmed platter or plates and cover to keep warm.

4 Pour in the brandy to de-glaze the frying pan. Allow the brandy to boil until it has reduced by half, scraping the base of the frying pan, then add the whipping cream and garlic. Bubble gently over a low-medium heat for about 4 minutes or until the cream has reduced by about one-third. Stir any accumulated juices from the meat into the sauce, taste and add salt as necessary. Serve the steaks hot, with the sauce.

LAMB CASSEROLE WITH GARLIC AND BEANS

This recipe has a Spanish influence and makes a substantial meal, served with potatoes.
Broad beans add colour and texture to the dish.

INGREDIENTS
45ml/3 tbsp olive oil
1.5kg/3–3½ lb lamb fillet, cut
into 5cm/2in cubes
1 large onion, chopped
6 large garlic cloves, unpeeled
1 bay leaf
5ml/1 tsp paprika
120ml/4fl oz/½ cup dry sherry
115g/4oz shelled fresh or frozen
broad beans
30ml/2 tbsp chopped fresh parsley
salt and freshly ground black
pepper

SERVES 6

3 Add the garlic, bay leaf, paprika and sherry. Season to taste and bring to the boil. Cover and simmer gently for 1½ hours, until tender.

4 Add the broad beans to the casserole and cook for a further 10 minutes. Stir in the chopped fresh parsley just before serving.

1 Heat 30ml/2 tbsp olive oil in a large flameproof casserole. Add half the meat and brown well on all sides. Transfer to a plate. Brown the rest of the meat in the same way and remove from the casserole.

2 Heat the remaining oil in the pan, add the onion and cook for about 5 minutes until soft. Return the meat to the casserole.

LAMB STEAKS MARINATED IN MINT AND SHERRY

*The marinade in this recipe is extremely quick to prepare and is the key
to its success: the sherry imparts a wonderful tang to the meat.*

INGREDIENTS

6 large lamb steaks or
12 smaller chops

FOR THE MARINADE
30ml/2 tbsp chopped fresh mint
leaves
15ml/1 tbsp black peppercorns
1 medium onion, chopped
120ml/4fl oz/½ cup sherry
60ml/4 tbsp extra virgin olive oil
2 garlic cloves

SERVES 6

1 Blend the mint leaves and
peppercorns in a food processor until
finely chopped. Add the onion and
process again until smooth. Add the
rest of the marinade ingredients and
process until completely mixed. The
marinade should be a thick consistency.

2 Add the marinade to the steaks or
chops and cover with clear film. Leave
in the fridge to marinate overnight.

3 Cook the steaks on a medium
barbecue for 10–15 minutes, basting
occasionally with the marinade.

STUFFED ROAST LOIN OF PORK

This recipe uses fruit and nuts as a stuffing for roast pork in the Catalan style. It is full of flavour and is very good served cold, making an excellent centrepiece for a summer buffet or a picnic.

INGREDIENTS

60ml/4 tbsp olive oil
1 onion, finely chopped
2 garlic cloves, chopped
50g/2oz/1 cup fresh breadcrumbs
4 ready-to-eat dried figs, chopped
8 stoned green olives, chopped
25g/1oz/¼ cup flaked almonds
15ml/1 tbsp lemon juice
15ml/1 tbsp chopped fresh parsley
1 egg yolk
900g/2lb boned loin of pork
salt and freshly ground black
pepper

SERVES 4

1 Preheat the oven to 200°C/400°F/ Gas 6, or prepare the barbecue. Heat 45ml/3 tbsp of the oil in a pan, add the onion and garlic, and cook gently until softened. Remove the pan from the heat and stir in the breadcrumbs, figs, olives, almonds, lemon juice, chopped fresh parsley and egg yolk. Season to taste with salt and ground black pepper.

2 Remove any string from the pork and unroll the belly flap, cutting away any excess fat or meat to enable you to do so. Spread the stuffing over the flat piece and roll it up, starting from the thick side. Tie at intervals with string.

3 Pour the remaining olive oil into a roasting tin and put in the pork, or arrange on the spit of the barbecue. Roast for 1 hour and 15 minutes, or until the juices run clear from the meat.

4 Remove the pork from the oven or the spit and, if serving hot, let it rest for 10 minutes before carving into thick slices. If serving cold, wrap the meat in foil to keep it moist until you carve it.

PORK WITH MARSALA AND JUNIPER

Sicilian Marsala wine gives savoury dishes a rich, fruity and alcoholic tang. The pork is fully complemented by the flavour of the sauce in this quick and luxurious dish.

INGREDIENTS

25g/1oz dried cep or porcini mushrooms
4 pork escalopes
10ml/2 tsp balsamic vinegar
8 garlic cloves
15g/½ oz/1 tbsp butter
45ml/3 tbsp Marsala
several rosemary sprigs
10 juniper berries, crushed
salt and freshly ground black pepper

SERVES 4

1 Put the dried mushrooms in a large bowl and just cover with hot water. Leave to stand for 20 minutes to allow the mushrooms to soak.

2 Brush the pork with 5ml/1 tsp of the vinegar and season with salt and pepper. Put the garlic cloves in a small pan of boiling water and cook for 10 minutes until soft. Drain and set aside.

3 Melt the butter in a large frying pan. Add the pork and fry quickly until browned on the underside. Turn the meat over and cook for 1 minute more.

4 Add the Marsala, rosemary sprigs, drained mushrooms, 60ml/4 tbsp of the mushroom water, the garlic cloves, juniper berries and the remaining balsamic vinegar.

5 Simmer gently for 3–5 minutes until the pork is cooked through. Season lightly and serve hot.

GRILLED CASHEW NUT CHICKEN

· · ·

This dish comes from the beautiful Indonesian island of Bali, where nuts are widely used as a base for sauces and marinades. Serve it with a green salad and a hot chilli dipping sauce.

INGREDIENTS

4 chicken legs
radishes, sliced, to garnish
1/2 cucumber, sliced, to garnish
Chinese leaves, to serve

FOR THE MARINADE
50g/2oz raw cashew or macadamia
nuts
2 shallots, or 1 small onion, finely
chopped
2 garlic cloves, crushed
2 small red chillies, chopped
5cm/2in piece lemon grass
15ml/1 tbsp tamarind sauce
30ml/2 tbsp dark soy sauce
15ml/1 tbsp Thai fish sauce
10ml/2 tsp sugar
2.5ml/1/2 tsp salt
15ml/1 tbsp rice or white wine
vinegar

SERVES 4

1 Using a sharp kitchen knife, slash the chicken legs several times through to the bone. Chop off the knuckle end and discard.

2 To make the marinade, place the cashew or macadamia nuts in a food processor or pestle and mortar and grind until fine.

3 Add the chopped shallots or onion, garlic, chillies and lemon grass and blend. Add the remaining marinade ingredients and blend again.

4 Spread the marinade over the chicken and leave for up to 8 hours in the fridge. Cook the chicken under a medium grill for 25 minutes, basting and turning occasionally. Garnish with radishes and cucumber and serve on a bed of Chinese leaves.

CHICKEN WITH FRESH HERBS AND GARLIC

A whole chicken can be roasted on a spit on the barbecue. This marinade keeps the flesh moist and delicious and the fresh herbs add summery flavours.

INGREDIENTS

1.75kg/4½ lb free-range chicken
finely grated rind and juice of 1
lemon
1 garlic clove, crushed
30ml/2 tbsp olive oil
2 fresh thyme sprigs
2 fresh sage sprigs
90ml/6 tbsp unsalted butter,
softened
salt and freshly ground black
pepper

SERVES 4

1 Season the chicken well. Mix the lemon rind and juice, crushed garlic and olive oil together and pour them over the chicken. Leave to marinate in the fridge for at least 2 hours.

Cook's Tip

If roasting the chicken in the oven, preheat the oven to 230°C/450°F/ Gas 8 and reduce the heat to 190°C/375°F/Gas 5 after 10 minutes. If you are roasting a chicken to serve cold, cooking it in foil helps to keep it succulent – open the foil for the last 20 minutes to brown the skin, then close it as the chicken cools.

2 Place the herbs in the cavity of the bird and smear the butter over the skin. Season well. Cook the chicken on a spit on the barbecue for 1½–1¾ hours, basting with the marinade, until the juices run clear when the thigh is pierced with a skewer. Leave the bird to rest for 15 minutes before carving.

SPICED DUCK WITH PEARS

° . °

This delicious casserole can be cooked on the barbecue or stove. The browned pears are added towards the end of cooking, along with a pine nut and garlic paste to flavour and thicken.

INGREDIENTS

6 duck portions, either breast or
leg pieces
15ml/1 tbsp olive oil
1 large onion, thinly sliced
1 cinnamon stick, halved
2 thyme sprigs
475ml/16fl oz/2 cups duck or
chicken stock

To FINISH
3 firm ripe pears, peeled and cored
30ml/2 tbsp olive oil
2 garlic cloves, sliced
25g/1oz/$\frac{1}{3}$ cup pine nuts
2.5ml/$\frac{1}{2}$ tsp saffron strands
25g/1oz/2 tbsp raisins
salt and freshly ground black
pepper
thyme sprigs or parsley, to garnish

SERVES 6

1 Fry the duck portions in olive oil for 5 minutes, until golden, or brush the portions with oil and cook them on a hot barbecue for 8–10 minutes, until golden. Transfer the duck to a large flameproof dish. If frying, drain off all but 15ml/1 tbsp of fat left in the pan.

2 Fry the onion in the frying pan for 5 minutes until golden. Add the cinnamon stick, thyme and stock and bring to the boil. Pour over the duck in the dish and cook slowly on a low barbecue for about 1¼ hours.

3 Halve the pears, brush with oil and barbecue until brown, or fry the pears in the oil on the hob. Pound the garlic, pine nuts and saffron with a pestle and mortar, to make a thick, smooth paste.

4 Add the paste, raisins and pears to the flameproof dish. Cook for 15 minutes until the pears are tender.

5 Season to taste and garnish with the fresh herbs. Serve with mashed potatoes and a green vegetable, if liked.

Cook's Tip
A good stock is essential for this dish. Buy a large duck (plus two extra duck breasts if you want portions to be generous) and joint it yourself, using the giblets and carcass for stock. If you buy duck portions, use a well-flavoured chicken stock.

STUFFED SARDINES

o o o

This Middle Eastern-inspired dish doesn't take much preparation and is a meal in itself.
Just serve with a crisp green salad tossed in a fresh lemon vinaigrette to make it complete.

INGREDIENTS

10g/¹/₄ oz fresh parsley

3–4 garlic cloves, crushed

8–12 fresh or frozen sardines,
prepared

30ml/2 tbsp lemon juice

50g/2oz plain flour

2.5ml/¹/₂ tsp ground cumin

olive oil, for brushing

salt and freshly ground black
pepper

naan bread and green salad,
to serve

SERVES 4

1 Finely chop the parsley and mix in a small bowl with the garlic. Pat the parsley and garlic mixture all over the outsides and insides of the prepared sardines. Sprinkle the sardines with lemon juice, then place them in a dish, cover and set aside in a cool place for up to 2 hours, to absorb the flavours.

2 Place the flour on a large plate and season with the cumin, salt and pepper. Roll the sardines in the flour.

3 Brush the sardines with olive oil and cook under a medium grill for about 3 minutes each side. Serve with naan bread and a green salad.

RED MULLET WITH LAVENDER

Barbecue a fish dish with a difference by adding lavender to red mullet for a wonderful aromatic flavour. Sprinkle some lavender flowers on the coals too, to give a delightful perfumed ambience.

INGREDIENTS

4 red mullet, scaled, gutted and cleaned
30ml/2 tbsp olive oil

FOR THE MARINADE
45ml/3 tbsp fresh lavender flowers or 15ml/1 tbsp dried lavender leaves, roughly chopped
roughly chopped rind of 1 lemon
4 spring onions, roughly chopped
salt and freshly ground black pepper

SERVES 4

1 Place the fish in a shallow dish. Mix the ingredients for the marinade and pour over the fish. Cover the fish with clear film and leave in the fridge to marinate for at least 3 hours.

2 Remove the fish from the marinade and brush it with olive oil. Cook the fish on a hot barbecue for about 10–15 minutes, turning once and basting with olive oil as it cooks.

BAKED APPLES IN HONEY AND LEMON

Tender baked apples with a classic flavouring of lemon and honey make a simple dessert.
Serve with custard or a spoonful of whipped cream, if you wish.

INGREDIENTS

4 medium cooking apples
15ml/1 tbsp honey
grated rind and juice of 1 lemon
15ml/1 tbsp butter, melted

SERVES 4

1 Preheat the oven to 200°C/400°F/ Gas 6. Core the apples, leaving them whole. Cut four squares of double thickness foil and brush with butter.

2 With a cannelle or sharp knife, cut lines through the apple skin at regular intervals.

3 Mix together the honey, lemon rind, juice and butter in a small bowl.

4 Spoon the mixture into the apples and wrap in foil, sealing the edges securely. Cook in the oven for 20 minutes, until the apples are tender.

POACHED PEARS IN MAPLE AND YOGURT SAUCE

This elegant dessert is easier to make than it looks – poach the pears on the hob or barbecue when you cook the main course, and have the cooled syrup ready to add just before serving.

INGREDIENTS

6 firm pears
15ml/1 tbsp lemon juice
250ml/8fl oz/1 cup sweet white
wine or cider
thinly pared rind of 1 lemon
1 cinnamon stick
30ml/2 tbsp maple syrup
2.5ml/¹/² tsp arrowroot
150ml/¹/⁴ pint/²/³ cup strained
Greek-style yogurt

SERVES 6

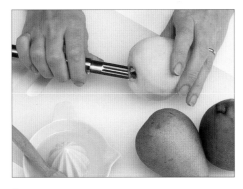

1 Peel the pears, leaving them whole and with stalks. Brush with lemon juice to prevent them discolouring. Use a potato peeler or small knife to scoop out the core from the base of each pear.

2 Place the pears in a wide, heavy pan and pour over the wine, with enough cold water to almost cover the fruit. Add the lemon rind and cinnamon stick, and bring to the boil on the hob or, using a flameproof pan, on the barbecue. Reduce the heat, cover and simmer for 30 minutes, or until tender. Lift out the pears carefully.

3 Boil the remaining liquid, uncovered, until reduced to about 120ml/4 fl oz/¹/² cup. Strain and add the maple syrup. Blend a little of the liquid with the arrowroot. Return to the pan and cook, stirring, until thick and clear. Allow to cool.

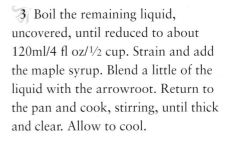

4 Slice each pear, leaving the slices attached at the stem end, and fan out on serving plates. Stir 30ml/2 tbsp of the cooled syrup into the yogurt and spoon around the pears. Drizzle the pears with the remaining syrup and serve immediately.

FRESH FIGS WITH VANILLA CREAM

The ripeness of the figs will determine their cooking time. This is an ideal recipe for a barbecue because it is prepared on the barbecue and left to stand until you are ready to eat.

INGREDIENTS
450ml/³⁄4 pint/scant 2 cups dry white wine
75g/3oz/¹⁄3 cup clear honey
50g/2oz/¹⁄4 cup caster sugar
1 small orange
8 whole cloves
450g/1lb fresh figs
1 cinnamon stick
sprigs of fresh mint, or bay leaves, to decorate

FOR THE VANILLA CREAM
300ml/¹⁄2 pint/1¹⁄4 cups double cream
1 vanilla pod
5ml/1 tsp caster sugar

SERVES 6

1 Put the wine, honey and caster sugar in a heavy saucepan and heat gently on the barbecue or hob until the sugar dissolves.

2 Stud the orange with the cloves and add to the syrup with the figs and cinnamon. Cover and simmer very gently for 5–10 minutes until the figs are tender. Transfer the contents of the pan to a serving dish and leave to cool.

3 Put 150ml/¹⁄4 pint/²⁄3 cup of the cream in a small saucepan with the vanilla pod. Bring almost to the boil, then leave to cool and infuse for 30 minutes. Remove the vanilla pod and mix the flavoured cream with the remaining cream and sugar in a bowl. Whip lightly. Transfer to a serving dish.

4 Decorate the figs with mint or bay leaves and serve with the vanilla cream.

CHOCOLATE MINT TRUFFLE FILO PARCELS

° ° °

These exquisite little parcels are utterly irresistible: there will be no leftovers. The use of fresh mint in the recipe gives a wonderfully fresh flavour.

2 Cut the filo pastry sheets into 7.5cm/3in squares and cover with a damp cloth to prevent them drying out.

3 Brush a square of filo with melted butter, lay on a second sheet, brush again and place a spoonful of filling in the middle of the top sheet. Bring in all four corners and twist to form a purse shape. Repeat to make 18 parcels.

4 Place the filo parcels on a griddle or baking sheet, well brushed with melted butter. Cook in the oven for about 10 minutes, until the filo pastry is crisp. Leave to cool, then dust lightly with sifted icing sugar and then with sifted cocoa powder.

INGREDIENTS

15ml/1 tbsp very finely chopped fresh mint
75g/3oz/³/4 cup ground almonds
50g/2oz plain chocolate, grated
115g/4oz/¹/2 cup crème fraîche or fromage frais
2 dessert apples, peeled and grated
9 large sheets filo pastry
75g/3oz/¹/3 cup butter, melted
15ml/1 tbsp icing sugar, to dust
15ml/1 tbsp cocoa powder, to dust

MAKES 18 PARCELS

1 Preheat the oven to 190°C/375F/ Gas 5. Mix the chopped fresh mint, almonds, grated chocolate, crème fraîche or fromage frais and grated apple in a large mixing bowl. Set aside.

HERBAL PUNCH

This refreshing party drink will have people coming back for more, and it is an original non-alcoholic choice for drivers and children.

INGREDIENTS
450ml/³/4 pint/scant 2 cups honey
4 litres/7 pints water
450ml/³/4 pint/scant 2 cups freshly
squeezed lemon juice
45g/3 tbsp fresh rosemary leaves,
plus extra to decorate
1.5kg/3¹/2 lb/8 cups sliced
strawberries
450ml/³/4 pint/scant 2 cups freshly
squeezed lime juice
1.75 litres/3 pints/7¹/2 cups
sparkling mineral water
ice cubes
3–4 scented geranium leaves

SERVES 30 PLUS

1 Combine the honey, 1 litre/ 1³/4 pints/4 cups water, one-eighth of the lemon juice and the fresh rosemary leaves in a saucepan. Bring to the boil, stirring, until the honey is dissolved. Remove from the heat and allow to stand for about 5 minutes. Strain into a large punch bowl and leave aside to cool.

2 Press the strawberries through a fine sieve into the punch bowl, add the rest of the water and lemon juice, the lime juice and the sparkling mineral water. Stir gently to combine the ingredients. Add the ice cubes just 5 minutes before serving, and float the geranium and rosemary leaves on the surface.

MINT CUP

Mint is a perennially popular flavouring and this delicate cup is a wonderful mixture with an intriguing taste. It is the perfect summer drink to serve with meals outdoors.

INGREDIENTS

handful fresh mint leaves
15ml/1 tbsp sugar
crushed ice
15ml/1 tbsp lemon juice
175ml/6fl oz/³/4 cup grapefruit juice
600ml/1 pint/2¹/2 cups chilled tonic water
mint sprigs and lemon slices, to decorate

SERVES 4–6

1 Crush the mint leaves with the sugar and put into a jug. Fill the jug to the top with crushed ice.

2 Add the lemon juice, grapefruit juice and tonic water. Stir gently to combine the ingredients and decorate with mint sprigs and slices of lemon.

STRAWBERRY AND MINT CHAMPAGNE

This is a simple concoction that makes a bottle of champagne or sparkling white wine go much further. It tastes very special on a hot summer's evening.

INGREDIENTS
500g/1¼lb strawberries
6–8 fresh mint leaves
1 bottle champagne or sparkling
white wine
fresh mint sprigs, to decorate

SERVES 4–6

2 Strain through a fine sieve into a large bowl. Half fill a glass with the mixture and top up with champagne or sparkling wine. Decorate with a sprig of fresh mint.

1 Purée the strawberries and fresh mint leaves in a food processor.

MELON, GINGER AND BORAGE CUP

Melon and ginger complement each other magnificently. If you prefer, you can leave out the powdered ginger – the result is milder but equally delicious.

INGREDIENTS
½ large honeydew melon
1 litre/1¾ pints/4 cups ginger beer
powdered ginger, to taste
borage sprigs with flowers,
to decorate

SERVES 6–8

1 Discard the seeds from the half melon and scoop the flesh into a food processor. Blend the melon to a purée.

2 Pour the purée into a large jug and top up with ginger beer. Add powdered ginger to taste. Pour into glasses and decorate with borage.

INDEX

° ° °

New Orleans steak salad, 26